Golfer mania

Cartoons by Wist

RAVETTE PUBLISHING

First Published by
Ravette Publishing Limited 1997

Printed and bound for
Ravette Publishing Limited,
Unit 3, Tristar Centre
Star Road, Partridge Green
West Sussex RH13 8RA

by Proost, Belgium

ISBN: 1 85304 932 8

Now, the 7th hole was the tricky one. Daddy's ball had landed right behind a tree, but I took my spoon and. . .

Was it on purpose you hit that little ball out in the lake, George?

Including the 4 children we had, it's been the best investment we ever made!

The picture became unsteady right in the middle
of next year's masters.

If I 'adn't been 'ere Guv'nor, you'd 'ave lost yer ball.
I grabbed it just as it was disappearin' down that 'ole.

Will you never learn not to ask your father how his golf
went, when he comes home early?

But isn't there anything else you can do in winter, when golfing is out of season, Herbie?

And please send me a driver and a crate of balls.

How long have your been with the firm, Jones?

When for once you do the washing-up, darling,
I wish you'd do it with good grace.

We could do with more of his type. See how
he stuck to his club tie to the last.

Shouldn't we forget about the ball, Sir, and try and find the course?

That's a new club record, guv'nor. Two and a 'alf twist.

Yes, yes, yes. But your ulcer will have to wait
until I've heard the results of the Open.

When you find the rule that says it's not permitted,
I'll take it off and not a moment before.

Oh blast! Three inches out again.

Relax. This isn't going to take long. . .

Have I or haven't I stayed at home to help you
in the garden – yes or no?

Isn't it about time you faced facts?
That drive of yours is hardly perfect.

Hurry up, Bill. There's no queue up at the 1st tee at all.

Excuse me. Are all the bunkers on this course as bad as this one?

Wrong again, Edwin. That's not the lawn-mower.

I said I'm sorry.

Is it today by any chance you're going
for a round of golf with the boys?

No thanks – I'm driving.

Well so far there's been no sign of life . . .

I've never been able to work out whether he's
overworked, plain lazy or out golfing.

Experience tells me, we'd better get to bed.

This is certainly the toughest course I've yet seen.

And the best bit about this game is that there seems to be no parking problems.

Well, . . . at least the direction was right, dear.

And I'd advise you not to play more than 27 holes
a day for the next couple of weeks.

Oh those! They're just something Herbie has won at some game or other.

What's new anyway old sport?

The nine iron please.

Are you trying to tell me you've had
a hole-in-one again, Herbert?

Remember the firm, steady grip, the rhythmic level stroke, and the smooth shoulder movement.

'Ere, guv'nor. Only 50 pence for my sensational
book: How To Be A Successful Golf-Pro.

I don't know what it is he's invented,
but he's never at home any more.

No, the General Manager went out about twenty minutes ago, but I'm expecting him back any minute!

Now, my good man, will you please get up. You're lying on my ball.

Quite, sir. But then everybody needs a good laugh now and then.

You didn't think that a wedding would take all day, did you?

All I can say is that I wouldn't care to go a round
with a fellow with that kind of temperament.

I say, don't you ever relax from your work, Sir?

Why, sure darling, you just pop into the club-house
and have a drink. It's your wedding, too.

We can't go on meeting like this, love.

Take a couple of aspirins, Mrs Jenkins and call me
again in a couple of hours if that hasn't helped.

This happens every time I get a putter into my hands, doctor.

Your first hole-in-one, I presume?

Of course this is the happiest day in my life,
darling. I could never afford a caddie before.

And on what grounds have you applied for one day's liberty, Jones?

They don't seem to be all that advanced. They just go around hitting small, white balls with some strange kind of sticks. . .

And finally, when you've perfected your drive, you run out of balls.

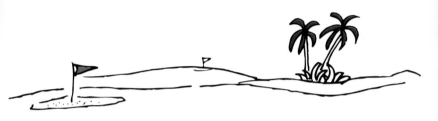

It's all right for you bachelors, you have only yourselves to think of. But I'll be ready at the crack of dawn.

Well, she wasn't too keen on it, but at long last she said I could go.